HOW TO BE A QUEEN

BY KATRINA RASBOLD

Published by Rasbold Ink
www.rasboldink.com

ISBN-13: 978-1500604516
ISBN-10: 1500604518

DEDICATION

This book is dedicated to all of the Queens out there, both of my own making and their own, plus those who don't yet know they are Queens. This is for you, sweethearts.

This book is especially dedicated to Linda Glascoe, who knows why.

Tremendous thanks to Kathy, Trish, Debby, Carolyn, and the other Queens and Men Who Love Royal Women who I featured in this book.

Thanks also to Jill Conner Browne who had the balls and the big hair to get on that float and show us all how it's done. I owe you so much, Boss Queen.

TABLE OF CONTENTS

INTRODUCTION

You will notice that the title of this book is not, *How to Become a Queen*. That is because if you pick up this book, you already pretty much know that you are a Queen and you want me – or anyone standing around with a clue in their back pocket – to validate that opinion for you. I am so very happy to do so. You might even just be hoping that someday you can step into your Queenly pumps and you want someone else to say, "No, not someday...*NOW*." If you already think you are a Queen, then you are. If you hope you are a Queen, then there you are: Queen.

Granted, it's not for everyone. There are handmaidens and loyal subjects and those who sit in the audience looking smug and pious and never really having any fun at all. You all know who they are and Lord knows, we don't want to be *they* but let me tell you, *they* are just as vital as Queens are to the matrix of society. We need staff and all, don't y'know.

This book is for those female-gendered persons who are trapped like a deer in headlights over the idea of grabbing hold of their own empowerment, putting it on their head, and wearing it out for a nice stroll. It's about how to reclaim your sovereign rights just on the off chance that you never had'em, never stretched'em, never activated'em, lost'em along the way, or worse yet, had some mind-bending asshole swipe them away from you all at once or a little bit at a time over years and years of wearing down. If you are holding this book, then I can *guarandamntee you* that it's time for you to snatch those things back and wear them like the crown jewels they are.

Throughout this book, you will notice a couple of things about how I speak and yes, the way I write in this book is, in fact, the way I speak to which anyone who knows me "in real life" can attest. One is that I am from the South and I speak as a true Southern woman. I have to admit to a particular degree of *"awwwww, poor darlin'"* feelings for people who are not from the South and do not have an authentic Southern accent. Such a thing goes far in the practice of being a Queen. For the love of the Goddess, do not attempt to fake one just to put it in your repertoire of Queenliness because trust me, it will only serve to detract from your Queenly credibility. I am quite sure your own voice will work just fine once you get some oomph behind it with your Queenly attitude. However, by all means, *find your voice*. It might be rusty and scratchy from lack of use, but girl, dig deep and get that bird to singing.

For more than half of my adult life, I was married to a man who occasionally made fun of my Southern accent and over time, I developed what my Mama called my "Sunday" voice which way very leveled and measured and only had a trace of accent to it. I can still do it when somebody asks me to. I hid behind that for a couple of decades, but when he eventually left me for an ugly woman (no accounting for taste and let me tell you, *that* karma came back for him with teeth worse than I *ever* would have inflicted on him) in the late nineties, I opened up my Southern accent for business again. I promised both myself and my Goddess right then and there that I would never again hide my drawling light under a bushel.

The other thing that you will notice is that I tend to swear from time to time. Well, OK, I swear *a lot*. As a writer, I love words and I do mean *all* words, but really, if I truly wrote the way I talk, the K would be worn off the K key on my keyboard. So yeah, I guess I do tone it down a bit and this book is my least toned down of them all

2

because in the other ones, I have to come off as scholarly and academic. Here...not so much.

CHAPTER 1 – RECLAIMING A BIRTHRIGHT DENIED

Very nearly every little girl wants to be a princess at some time in her childhood and companies like Disney capitalize on this dream through their "Disney Princess" line of movies and the accompanying accessory line of costumes and play items. Unfortunately, it does not take long at all for the world to strip us of that delightful fantasy and presume we will never pursue it again. In fact, the world works aggressively at making certain that we will *never* feel Queenly and regal by undermining our confidence at every turn. That is why the weight loss industry is a multi-zillion dollar proposition and hair and make-up companies aren't doing too shabby either. We are taught from early on that how we look, how we act, how we think, and who we are on our own are not acceptable to society. Our purpose in the world, based on the input we receive from the media and people around us is to be useful, quiet, and proper.

You have heard all of the complaints. A man who tells people what to do has great leadership skills and is an alpha male. A woman who tells people what to do is a bitch. A man who goes after what he wants is on the fast track. A woman is a gold-digger or a femi-Nazi. We have made such great strides since the time of the suffragists, but assertiveness and confidence in females can still raise the rancor of our Western culture.

Consider the comments of Republican Representative from North Caroline, Renee Elmers, who said:

"Men do tend to talk about things on a much higher level. Many of my male colleagues, when they go to the House floor, you know, they've got some pie chart or graph behind them and they're talking about trillions of dollars and how, you know, the debt is awful and, you know, we all agree with that. [...] We need our male colleagues to understand that if you can bring it down to a woman's level and what everything that she is balancing in her life – that's the way to go."

Even from within our own ranks, we are made to appear as dithering idiots whose minds are completely blown by a pie chart and who say, "...you know..." as punctuation. It's as though our little feather heads just cannot fathom the idea that the debt is a big awful thing that must be somehow managed (*you know*).

Just because there are fundamental differences in how males and females process information does not mean that we are stupid and it is time for more of us to step into our rightful roles as intelligent, calm, powerful people. This happens when we go back to our royal roots and reclaim our sovereign right to reign supreme.

Some of us get to continue living out princess fantasies through the idea of being "Daddy's Little Princess," but there comes a time, usually around puberty (purity balls aside - *full body shudder*), when that just gets creepy and societal norms require us to abandon our dreams of royalty. We begin to get the message from the people around us that despite what our hearts tell us, not only are we not royalty, *we are not even all that special*. We are *ordinary* and have no right to feel high and mighty. If we are anything other than ordinary, then it's a bad thing that must be stopped...*immediately*.

The natural progression from "Princess" as we age is to step into our royal shoes as "Queen," but how many of us ever get to do that? We buy into the lie that takes our birthright away and we believe the myth that we cannot be Queens. That is where the real tragedy begins. We start to crawl into, or else get shoved kicking and screaming into, our appropriate pigeonholes of "nerd," "brain," "basket case," "dweeb," "sidekick," "loser," "slut," "druggie," etc. As we age, we then hear "breadwinner," "cougar," "old maid," "soccer mom," "gold-digger," "barfly," "welfare queen" (now there's some royalty right there), "Barbie doll," "trophy wife," and so on. When we are told who we are enough times, in absence of support for who we know ourselves to be, we will usually begin to believe the consensus.

As we age, we experience few moments to be the royal self that blossomed inside the dreams of that little girl who was, for a short time, a princess. Only a handful of females ever get to reign as Homecoming Queen and then it is typically the most popular, attractive, and wealthy girls in school who wear the crown and sash. By the time we are in the last two years of high school, most of us who are not in the higher crust of academic society already gave up on aspiring to such greatness. We know we will not be any of the superlatives in the yearbook; at least not any of the flattering ones.

Many women get to be "Queen for a Day" on their wedding day, which ends up being one of the last or only times in their lives they will get to wear the crown and rule supreme in their adult lives unless they take action on their own to do so. Is it any wonder that women plan their wedding day in their minds, months, or even years before they meet the man they will marry? Is there any wonder some women walk down the aisle so many times? Is it any wonder some women get so caught up in the idea of having a

wedding that they fail to fully consider the implications of having a marriage? Is it any wonder that many women turn into "bridezillas" and abuse everyone around them if the moment is not perfect or their wedding ideal is threatened in some way? With so few rites of passage in our civilized life, we cling to the ones we are granted and certainly to the ones that allow us to wear a tiara.

Little boys do not face this crisis of aspirations for the most part. Having raised five of them to rather subjective maturity, I can say with a degree of assurance that most little boys do not dream of being royalty and so their dreams remain achievable goals. If a little boy fantasizes about being an astronaut or a firefighter or a police officer or a racecar driver, he has the option of seeking out the appropriate training and fulfilling his dream. If a woman dreams of being a Queen, even Queen of Her Own Life, she is laughed back into the kitchen.

Little girls just have to suck it up...*or so we are told.*

What if an alternative plan presented and we could be Queens all the time, every day, just as we imagined when we were younger? Our dream of being a princess or a Queen was taken away from us by the harsh lies of a world that tell us that only a scarce few will ever get to wear a crown. We believed it because we trusted the people who were smarter than we were at the time. The reality is really very simply and is the best-case scenario we can imagine: *those people were mistaken.* Any of us can be Queens. We just have to step up and claim our crown because let me tell you, Sweetheart, ain't nobody else going to do it for us and that's the Goddess's own truth. WE are responsible for taking that baby back.

The beauty is that when you claim this crown, you get all the glory and none of the hardship that a Queen by heredity gets. For us, being a Queen does not mean public appearances you don't want to make or obligatory photo ops on the lawn with your children. It doesn't mean being on the stick (innuendo intended) to produce an heir and any number of "spares" if you choose not to. You don't have to sling a single bottle of Champaign against the side of a boat (alcohol abuse, I tell you) or cut a single ribbon with giant scissors or give Christmas speeches. Of course, if either Elizabeth or Kate happens to be reading this, yes...for you it does mean this.

For most, however, being a Queen means being Queen of Your Own Life. You fully invest in every moment, you reject the factors that cause you stress and unhappiness, and you take full responsibility for your personal joy. You make a conscious choice to nurture your own pleasure first, which then leaves you filled up and overflowing to give to others. It starts with baby steps, and then blossoms into a lifestyle before you know it.

The first step is the hardest, but once you put your royal foot forward and move, you step over into a whole new world.

CHAPTER 2 - HOW I FOUND OUT I WAS A QUEEN (A LITTLE HISTORY)

It makes sense that you would think that being all Queenly like I am that I was always this way. Truth be told, you would not have recognized me twenty or thirty years ago and quite honestly, when I have regrettable moments of reverting, you would not recognize me now. One of my dearest friends and Queen Sisters just very recently had to drop the bullshit flag and kick my own ass all over Denny's because I lost my perspective and let someone else take away my dignity. It happened a little at a time, so I did not notice it as much, but let me tell you, it happened and if it happened to *a seasoned Queen like myself*, it can happen to you too and maybe already has. Either way, it's never too late and that is why you have to do like any other Queen does *and have people*. Specifically, you have to have people who will tell you when you are driving your pumpkin coach into a giant ditch (or off a cliff). People keep you in line and on the throne doing the princess wave. If you don't have people, it's easy to lose your perspective very quickly.

I have always said that if you live in Crazy Town long enough, they will make you the mayor (do *not* aspire to be Queen of Crazy Town). When you care about someone and are in a relationship with them, over time, stuff you know to be inaccurate about yourself or about the world starts to sound like truth when you hear it enough times. You can begin to doubt yourself, your own sanity, and your own wisdom when someone you love and respect routinely shouts you down and contradicts you. Again, this is why we need other people we trust to let us know that we are going astray. It took me a very long time to realize that I was so far off the Queenly path and it was quite by accident that I found my way back again, with the exception of occasional detours such as the one I mentioned a couple of paragraphs ago.

However, I digress and back we go to the real grass roots of the Queen thing.

In 2006, two big things happened in Grizzly Flats, California. One was that we had our first Christmas parade and the other was the birth of the Queens of Grizzly Flats. My friend, Marcia (that's "Mar-see-ah", not "Marsha" like "Brady") suggested/demanded that I read a book called *The Sweet Potato Queens' Book of Love.* In it, the author, my own Boss Queen, Jill Conner Browne, talks about how she never got to ride on parade floats or be Homecoming Queen her own self and how she was just sick to death of it. To wit, when the Jackson, Mississippi St. Patrick's Day Parade happened many years ago, she made herself a float and hopped right up on it and just started waving.

After I picked up the little bitty bits of my brain that exploded all over my chaise lounge where I was reading this brilliant idea, I phoned Marcia and said, "You do know we're doing this at the Grizzly Flats Christmas Parade, right?"

Her reply? "How soon can we go thrift shopping for sequins?"

The answer was "Soon" and yes we sure did.

We put on big hair, stuffed our fronts and our backs, put on our sequins (all but my daughter, Delena, who refused to wear them, but got to ride with us none-the-less), and crawled up into the back of my husband's old white mining pickup truck which we had decorated to high Heaven. Delena's friend, Emily, did not dress up, but did sit on our truck and played the theme song from "The Legend of Zelda"on a pennywhistle for us. All through the parade, we waved just like we were royalty and we threw Hershey's kisses (Get it? Throwing kisses?) and said, "Whoooo hooo!" to people and smiled like our faces were going to break.

We took a real risk that we'd be laughed out of town on a stick, but let me tell you, *everyone loved us!* I shit you not when I tell you that old men *ran after us* having seen the sign on our truck yelling "We love you, Grizzly Flats Queens!"

When we dismounted after the parade, we had a flock of people around us wanting to touch our stuffed butts and boobs and of course, feel our big hair. It was glorious and Marcia and I got more attention than we knew what to do with and loved every minute of it. Delena didn't get as much because she was young and not given to dressing up like we were, plus people could go to jail for checking her out like they were doing to us.

Honestly, I never expected such a reaction, especially considering that many of the people here on the mountain are a little, well... *uckstay upnay.* I did hear that one of our more pious residents sort of did a nose-in-the-air thing about how *anyone* would want to humiliate themselves in such a way. For myself, I'd rather shag my fat ass up onto a parade float and have elderly groupies chase after me down the road than to be a haughty old biddy who doesn't know how to have any fun.

Have fun we did and for the forty-five minutes or so that we were on the float, it was a Queenly sisterhood. We gathered in a reverent amalgam of big hair (higher the hair, closer to Jesus, OH HELL YEAH!), sequins, perfume, cat-eye glasses, opera gloves, and sunshine.

Mother Jill, our Boss Queen, would have been proud.

The first two Grizzly Flats Queens, me and Marcia (on the left).

By the time the next Grizzly Flats parade rolled around on Independence Day, we had tons of women just absolutely pleading and begging us to let them be Queens right along with us. We figure a big part of it was the artificial baby seal stoles we wore at Christmas to keep warm. I mean, who wouldn't want one? We had no idea it was going to blow up like that, but it sure did and we knew we had a situation on our hands. (Note: No real or fake baby seals were harmed in the making of our stoles).

We sussed out what we thought to be the most invested candidates and we set about planning our queenly procession for the July 4th parade. We were well and truly Queens and we were moving up in the world.

Over the years, our Queen events ceased. There is only so much fabulousness that a little town can take. I think we would all have liked for it to continue on forever, but the non-profit organization that ran the parade went royal tits up and there were no more parades. We are all still Queens in our hearts and in our lives, but now we wear our tiaras on the inside instead of the outside.

For the time it went on, however, it was popular and I highly recommend that anyone who is interested, just give it a try. It definitely wakes up the ego in a very necessary way and if you have to start your own damned parade to make it happen, baby, bring out those fire trucks and start the confetti flying. It is well worth the effort. In the photo that follows, you see our July 4th line up and by then, Queenmania was such that we had to have a manager and a driver, as you can see. They made sure everyone around us was respectful and gracious except mostly for us. They couldn't wrangle us if they tried and they knew better than to try.

The Grizzly Flats parades went on for a few years and the Queens of Grizzly Flats were always the hit of the season. By the time the next Christmas rolled around, just a short year after Marcia and I boldly crawled up into the back of our pickup truck all on our own, we had Santa himself asking to pose with us because we were all so beautiful. Good thing he had that roomy white fluff at his waist...I'm just sayin'...

This is part of our Queenly entourage that same year.

We put in Queenly appearances for Easter in our finery:

The next July 4th we celebrated our independence from the shackles of Queen suppression.

And the men still ran after us.

My point is that we were not Queens because of the families to which we were born or the country we lived in or because the school student body voted for us. We became the Queens of Grizzly Flats, California *just because we said so*. The beauty of it is that no one even questioned us about it; they just accepted that we were the Queens *as well they should*.

That time showed me in aces how coveted a position it was to be Queen of pretty much anything. I saw how damned easy it was to arrange and how eager the whole wide world was to accept our self-appointed sovereignty. After that, I pretty much made it my life's mission to get as many women as possible - and yes, a few men - to metaphorically climb up on that parade float with me, put on their tiaras and their sequins, and proclaim themselves to be Queens. They loved it...and guess what? So can you.

It reminded me of a time when my husband was a very young man in the US Air Force stationed in Korea and he got froggy and jumped up onto a stripper pole and started doing his thang with the pole. The guys he was with jeered and laughed and made fun, but you know what? They were watching *him* and he was having fun. For all of their macho bullshit, I will bet nearly all of them *wished* they had the balls to do what he did. Being a Queen is about finding your balls, engaging life instead of sitting on the sidelines, and getting up on that stripper pole.

How do you do it? Don't worry a moment, darlin', because that is what this book is all about. Without wasting precious pre-Queen time, here are 10 steps to take you there.

(You're welcome)

CHAPTER 3 – STEP 1: SAY IT LOUD, SAY IT PROUD, SAY IT OFTEN, AND MEAN IT WHEN YOU SAY IT

Your proclamation will feel strange at first, so it is best to practice it in the mirror for a while until you can speak the words with confidence. I recommend doing so even before you buy your tiara because then you will feel kind of breathlessly confident the first time you say it while wearing your crown. Trust me, it makes a difference.

"Hello. My name is Queen [insert your name here]. I am the Queen of [insert your domain here]." I have found that saying "Everything" as what you are Queen of is very damned effective, especially if you put a little bite in your voice as you say it. In fact, say it a bunch of times.

You can enter a skill or area of genius you possess or you can say something vague like "Queen of Quite a Lot" or "Queen of The World." It matters not; just say it with pride and conviction and such a big smile that no one will ever dare question it in a million years.

Say things that you would normally consider arrogant and over-the-top like, "Because I am the Queen, that's why." "Brang me my tiara!" (In this case, it helps to alter the pronunciation to phonetically as "Tie-Are-Uh.") If you feel peckish, you can say things like, "Talk to the scepter, bitches" and "We are not amused."

Do you see why you have to practice? It can be a challenge to work those types of comments into conversation and you will likely feel very awkward doing so, but it is sort of like when a dog pisses around an area to mark it as his own. You're marking your own identity and claiming it. Sure, "they" may titter and roll their eyes, but under it all, you'd better believe that "they" are hard at work acquiescing and genuflecting. The bottom line is that if you truly believe it, everyone else will believe it too. The trick is that YOU have to believe it first.

You are going to feel *stupid as hell* when you first say it *because "they" have taught you to feel stupid*. We are conditioned to feel unimportant and without regal standing. We might be vital to certain processes. We may be *capable* and *necessary*. Are we, however, *royalty*? That takes some getting used to for all concerned. (The answer is, "Yes. Yes, we are.")

Every day, make it a practice to *verbally* claim your sovereignty by saying things like, "I am Queen of All I Survey." "I am Queen of My Office, so sayeth me!" "I am Queen of Mulberry Street, oh hell yes, I am." When you have done this for a few days and start to nestle down into the idea, go on and start saying it to other people. Do not give them a prelude like, "I'm about to whip out some heavy shit on you, so don't laugh and make me feel bad." You just jump right in there with your "Because I'm the Queen and I will have your head if you fail to comply." Then give them a meaningful stare, flip your hair, and move along. It gives them something to think very hard about for a good twenty minutes or so and that's never a bad thing.

Your words have power and your voice deserves to be heard. Your words are the conduit to your will and without your will you truly are the "nothing" *they* want you to believe that you are.

Too many women have forgotten how to want. They get so caught up in the needs of their family, either the ones they birthed or the ones that birthed them or both. They get so immersed in the needs of their office or their community or their church or whatever other big-ass, all encompassing, soul-sucking black hole they have that they forget how to want anything for themselves. How often is a woman asked, "What do you want for your birthday" and they answer with, "Oh, I don't know. You don't have to get me anything!" *What. The. Hell?* Don't GET me anything for my BIRTHDAY? When this comes out of your mouth, you are having a severe Queen emergency.

If someone cares enough about you to ask what you want for your birthday or Mother's Day or Christmas, they are likely going to get you something anyway and rather than risk some shitty present that you want to immediately re-gift but instead shove in the closet in case they ask about it later, *give them options.* Get the stuff you want! Keep a list going of material desires in a variety of price ranges. Consider abstract gifts such as services (prepare me a home cooked meal, clean my house, watch my kids, give me a manicure, give me a massage), but good lord, *tell them something!*

I have a friend, one of the Grizzly Flats Queens, in fact, who became extremely ill. Another of the Queens phoned to ask her what she needed and she kept saying, "Really, I don't need anything" and honestly, maybe she didn't. Nonetheless, the friend who was not sick showed up at her house with homemade soup. When the sick friend protested, the not sick friend said, "Did you ever consider that maybe *this* is *my* ministry?"

People enjoy doing things for other people and too often, we get so caught up in being capable, important, strong, and independent that we refuse to allow others the pleasure of caring for us, which in turn, robs us of the pleasure of letting someone care for us. Likewise, we often leave others baffled as to what they could possible give to us that is of any value if we insist on always being stalwart and refuse help from everyone. How can *they* have value in our life if we insist on doing everything? We have to allow others to care for us and to see that we have needs as well. This is especially true in our children. How do we show them that *our* time is valuable and that we need help from them if we do not allow openings for that to happen?

It is a popular practice to say that when we have children, we must sacrifice our own wants and needs in consideration of the fact that we chose to procreate. While this is reasonable to a point, we must still teach children that although they are precious, they are not the center of the world every single minute of every single day. Sometimes, they must have patience and wait. Sometimes, what they want is not going to happen not because there is a reasonable explanation, but simply because *I am tired and do not want to drive you to the mall right now*. As I used to say to my daughter, "Sometimes, the answer is just 'no.'"

Sadly, the world is not set up in such a way as to give us all we want. While I understand and accept the idea that as parents, we

22

can shield kids from that harsh reality to a certain degree, to raise them in a bubble that tells them that their wants and needs supersede those of others sets them up for some serious life lessons when they get out into the "real" world.

Most people cannot read your mind and there is a tendency to overestimate the ability of those around us to understand what we need or want. Use your Queen voice and spell it out. It's easy to say, "Ask for what you want," but the precursor to that is *knowing what you want* and that might take some practice, just like saying Queenly things. Get in touch with what you want and let others around you know. It is then up to them to provide that or not. If they fail to do so, find a way to provide it for yourself.

That sounds counter-intuitive because if you are a Queen, others need to be doing *for you*, right? They will, but they can't do so if they don't know what you need and want, so you have to tell them and be very direct. Don't imagine for a minute that they can take a hint or read between the lines. Risk no such ambiguity. You have to tell them directly and use little words so they get it.

If wanting stuff feels foreign to you or you find you don't know how to want anymore, start out small with a little list. Think of five or six things you want. It doesn't matter what it is. It can be things like, "I want some bubble bath," "I want a back rub," or "I want someone else to sweep the floors today." Just think of something nice whether you actually want it or not, then tell folks and watch what happens. Say things like, "You know, I would just love it if you would..." If they scoff (and sometimes, they might), just get a faraway and slightly crazy look on your face and say, "That's fine. I'll remember that and I will find someone else to do it for me," then walk away and don't look back, even if it's just into the next room. Let them stew on that for a while.

This will take some work for some of you, especially if you don't yet really have the crazy eyes down. As a word of warning: Don't practice crazy eyes in the mirror. You'll whammy yourself

If you can't find anyone to do any of the things on your list then A) You truly need to do them for yourself and B) You need to start hanging around a different class of people because *damn*. There is also C) Screw it because you deserve a break. If no one will sweep your floors that day, then just leave those nasty things unswept. (Yes, really) If anyone complains, tell them they are welcome to pick up the broom, then go back to reading your magazine ("Queens Today"). Now, here's another brief word of warning:

The "deer caught in headlights" look and distinct discomfort with wearing the tiara that Queen Carolyn is demonstrating in the previous photo shows the typical characteristics of someone who has not fully embraced their Queenliness and found confidence in their royal Jimmy Choos. Mind you, this is purely for educational purposes only and I assure you, Queen Carolyn is regal in every way *without fail* both then and now.

Until the Queen energy truly begins flowing with great force through your precious little kundalini, you are going to feel moments of self-doubt and insecurity. You are going to wonder what entitles *you* to be in charge and why *you* should get what you want in life. Just push all those stupid thoughts away. They are the echoes of your old life put in place by a society that wants you to stay very controllable and useful to them.

It takes time to keep the internal Queen voice strong and solid and *that is why you have to practice.* Some women are naturals, such as Queen Debby, the first photo in this chapter. That was her first time to wear a tiara and she was working it. For some, it takes longer for it to sink in, so you have to practice, practice, and PRACTICE! As you can see, the results of getting out into the world and walking your Queenliness around prematurely can be tragic. There may be times it backfires, but you have to get right up, act as if you meant to do that, put your royal nose in the air and walk away with royal indignation all around you. The words, "I mean to do that!" are tremendously valuable. Make any misstep part of the Queenly dance.

You have to give yourself some good mirror time in the beginning and that starts with actually *looking* at yourself in the mirror, into your own eyes, and forgiving that person for the mistakes they made. Work on that for a bit, then straighten up your crown and go for a walk because you know what? Screw'em.

CHAPTER 4 – STEP 2: DON'T YOU EVEN BELIEVE THEM

As I alluded to in the previous chapter, there is always a chance that the people around you are not going to be particularly supportive of your newly embraced confidence and grandiose sense of entitlement. This is particularly true if you got kicked around for a while and have kissed a lot of ass your life. Those who benefit from your tenure as a service person occasionally respond poorly to the idea that some of your energy is now going for your own pursuits and Goddess bless'em, *they'll be OK*. Let them grieve and adjust to the change and before long, everyone will appreciate the happier you so much, they won't even care anymore. Just give it some time and let them adapt. Of course, you may have to endure a tantrum or two in the meantime, but just smile and tell them to get back to you when they are finished, then walk away. As a Queen, a timely exit speaks volumes.

There will also be some people, and sadly to say, it's often female people, who look at you walking your new confident, happy self around and think or even say out loud, *"Who does that uppity bitch think she is?"*

Many more of us than want to admit it care deeply about the opinions others hold of us and getting over *that* fatal flaw is one of the first and most essential steps to moving into full Queen status. Remember that just like the sniffy woman who scoffed at us being on the parade float, *these are the people who wish they had the nerve to get on the stripper pole.* They are the spectators who are no more than the audience to life. They sit on the sidelines and criticize those people who get out there, plug in, and live life. Most of all, you cannot let people *like that* take away your joy and your entitlement to respect and happiness. If all the world is a stage, then we certainly need an audience, 'tis true. Audiences can be brutal, but nonetheless, I'd rather be on the stage participating than sitting on my ass in the stadium seat.

Plenty of people are going to be on hand to tell you how you ought to be and how you ought not to be. Women who stand up for themselves, who take up space in the world, and who are unwilling to be a doormat or an energy ATM for everyone around them are often looked upon with disdain. Somewhere over time, the ability to resist letting people take advantage of you became a sin rather than a grace.

When the naysayers start braying like donkeys, ridiculing, questioning, and trying to knock you off your pedestal, **girl, don't you listen!** The hard truth is that if someone truly cannot look beyond their own selfish wants long enough to allow you to have some self-esteem, then you don't need to have them around and if you *have* to have them around because you gave birth to them or something, then they have got to be retrained, *pronto.*

Despite what you may have been taught in your life, you are under no obligation, no matter who you married, birthed, or befriended, to have to set your life up in service to other people. Sure, there are obligations we attend and honor, but our whole world does not have to turn on the whim of any person. We do not have to serve a life sentence for loving someone and we ARE entitled to pursuing our own happiness despite what any jackass might say. We can find balance in doing what we have to do while still claiming our own rights, our own freedoms, and our own joys.

Flack for being a Queen comes in many forms. Sometimes, it is the women around you who are not yet ready to break out and claim their place in their own monarchy who are the meanest when you make efforts to stand up for yourself and claim what is yours. It can be hard to watch someone step up and take what you yourself are afraid to have and those people are just in that place. They would rather talk down the person who is making positive changes and refusing to take shit off anyone anymore. This is an excellent time to learn who your real friends are and who are just around for what you can give them or do for them. Your real friends are the ones who applaud your efforts toward Queenliness and say things like "It's about time!" and "You go, girl!!"

Now this is not to say that one should make a fool of oneself. You do not have to be loud, brassy, and trashy and of course, no one would ever expect a true Queen to be those things. A Queen commands with her quiet, strong disposition. No, you do not have to be stern, but firm is often a requirement.

Sometimes, the dissension comes from those people who you no longer allow to bleed you completely dry for their own selfish gain. A little while before I learned how to be a Queen, I had a dream that was very telling. I was walking down a non-descript, but very long dirt path. I was tired and hungry and could barely put one foot in front of the other. I had no food. I had no water. I had no strength. From out of nowhere, I was overrun by a pack of creatures that looked sort of like weasels and had sharp little teeth. They managed to pull me down onto the ground and then they were all over me, chewing and gnawing with those little needle teeth, pulling off hunks of flesh and making all sorts of happy sounds as they ate me. Very quickly, I stopped resisting and fighting them off and just let them eat, feeling grateful that I could give of myself to them, even though the pain was tremendous. When I was nothing but a skeleton, they skittered away and left me there.

This dream exactly reflects where I was in my life at that time. I would give everything I had away to whoever wanted it and thank them for taking it. Hint: *Don't do this.*

Alas! The time will come when *someone* will work up the nerve to question you about why you are wearing a tiara or why you think you're all that. It is essential that you realize that these people would give absolutely anything to have the yarbles to do what you are doing and they are acting out of pure white-hot jealousy. While mercy is a wonderful Queenly virtue that we should bestow in abundance, Dr. Phil does assert that we have to teach people how to treat us and these envious doubters need to schooled *immediately.*

Regain your royal composure quickly and give them "the look" (as Queen Kathy and Queen Trish are perfectly executing in the previous photo) and then smile your biggest smile and make them feel foolish for asking.

A woman once asked me with a bit of a sneer to her voice, "How come you're wearing a tiara?" I immediately turned on her with a "Who touched the hem of my garment?" look and said, "Sweetheart, the real question is why aren't YOU wearing one?" She shut right up and became my #1 fan. Just like in the prison yard dynamic, how you respond to a challenge can define you as a Queen... or not.

These types will quickly return to wishing fervently that they were you if you just make them feel simple and stupid for saying such a dumbass thing in the first place.

CHAPTER 5 – STEP 3: NO NEGATIVE SELF-TALK

Many of the women who do the work to become Queen of Their Own Lives would never talk about another person using the horrible language they speak in their own internal dialogue. For instance, let's explore some very telling questions that are part of your self-talk. Do you have thousands of digital photos of your family and only a handful of yourself because you deleted them all because you did not like how you look? Do you have a bad day if you do not see the numbers you want to see when you step on the scale that morning? Do you say things like, "I am such an idiot!" or "I can't do *anything* right." "I don't deserve to be loved because I am fat." "I don't want to see photos of myself because I always look terrible." "I am not smart, so I can't take that job." "I am too old to go out and have fun." "I am a mother, so I have to sacrifice so my children can have what they want." "I owe everything I am and all that I have to my family." "My husband/boyfriend will not love me if I do not ___." "Oh, he would never allow me to…"

If so, I am going to pull you up short right there and demand that you give yourself the love, respect, and credit that you so fully deserve. Whoever you are, whatever you have done, whomever you have hurt in your life, and whoever has hurt you, you are worthy. You can be here. You can have air, water, and food. You can take up space. You can stand tall. You matter. What you want and need is important and is no less important than what other people want or need. You do NOT have to sacrifice everything for others and you absolutely do NOT have to give someone else the power to tell you what you are and are not "allowed" to do when you are a grown-ass woman.

If you accidentally got yourself into one of those situations, it is time to start extricating yourself by changing the dynamic.

One thing a Queen does better than anyone else is to monitor her energy flow and keep enough of that precious juice in reserve so that she lives a vibrant, healthy, plugged-in life. As you well know, as soon as our own well runs dry, we are no longer fun to be around, we begin to give over into despair and resentment, we lose our zest for life, and we have trouble enjoying anything. All of the color leaves our faces, our complexions get all pasty, and we have resting bitchface all the time. While that may decrease laugh-lines and crinkles, it is bad for the spirit and very definitely toxic to our interpersonal relationships. Remember that if you leave the world without laugh lines, you did not laugh enough and that is a real tragedy.

When we are in a bad place and do not give ourselves opportunities to thrive and step into our most authentic selves, we rarely have anything nice to say to or about ourselves. We see ourselves as tools with no purpose other than to work toward the fulfillment of other people. We use negative self-talk throughout our day.

Let me tell you a solid truth. Whatever you put out there into the world, whatever you are saying about yourself, the world will believe completely. If you tell yourself that you aren't loveable, that you are a loser, that you can't do anything right, that you are stupid or worthless, the world will say, "You must be right! I believe you!" You will attract (true story) experiences that validate that opinion. You will draw in as though magnetized people who will treat you as though you are unlovable, you are a loser, you can't do anything right, and you are stupid and worthless. When you say, "I am surrounded by users and drama queens," the world says, "I see and understand. Here y'go. You are surrounded by users and drama queens, sure enough" and then you get a whole wad more of them. For the record, those are a kind of queen we *do not* want to be. Notice that it does *not* get a capital letter.

The world around you works on an energy level and words and thoughts are measurable energy. The world responds to the energy you put out there. Energy does *not* understand a negative connotation. It hears only nouns and verbs, subjects, predicates, direct objects, and subjective complements. Nothing else. So if you say, "I want no more assholes in my life," what it hears is "I – want – assholes." It hears the noun (I), the verb (want) and the direct object (assholes). All of the rest of the sentence components turn into so much verbal trash and gets discarded.

This is why it is so very important to focus on what you *do* want to happen rather than what you *do not* want to happen. Self-help books instruct us to "focus on the positive!" and there is a very sound esoteric reason for that. What we focus on is what will grow.

This is why affirmations work so very well even though they sound so very dorky. Energy is created through word and intent and it goes out into the world with a specific purpose. It is targeted to a particular result and the energy flows along the path of least resistance very well. There are no negatives to navigate around and no flowery, extraneous language to circumnavigate. It is a solid, direct flow to the world.

I am beautiful.

I attract money.

I am worthy of love.

I welcome abundance.

I radiate joy.

I am healthy and strong.

I am wise and thoughtful.

I am sexy and vibrant.

I have enough.

My spirit soars.

Just...bam... get right to the intent. I run a group dedicated to positive manifestation and we call this practice, "Name it and claim it." Act as though it is already so before it is.

Many people swear they have a positive self-image, yet have no idea how often they create negative thoughts and words about themselves. Promise yourself that for a minimum of one week, you will be very, very aware of all thought and word energy that you put out into the world, especially regarding yourself and your life.

Another aspect of negative self-talk is, for the love of the Grand Goddess, *stop apologizing for everything!* Studies repeatedly demonstrate that women apologize far more than men do. I hear women apologize *when someone else bumps into THEM*, when they need to ask a reasonable question, or when they tell someone 'no.' I know women who apologize at least fifteen or twenty times a day. Are they truly "wrong" that often? It is as though they must apologize simply for taking up space in the world. Remember that when we say, "I'm sorry" all the time for every encumbrance real and imagined, it diminishes the impact when we truly do need to say that we are sorry for wronging someone. Knock it off.

You words have power. Do not use that power to push your own life and self-esteem further into the ditch.

CHAPTER 6 – STEP 4: KEEP YOUR SIDE OF THE STREET CLEAN

This is such a tough issue for Queens and non-royals alike. We do not have to be above reproach as nearly all ruling dynasties have shown over time, but it certainly helps our credibility if we take full ownership both of our responsibilities and our mistakes and work graciously to successfully manage both atonement and self-betterment. It all sounds daunting until you really stop and think about what is yours to manage and what is not. That cleans things up considerably and lightens the load almost every time.

You've probably heard the phrase, "Not my circus; not my monkeys." It is essential in order to be a whole and grounded person that you are very, very clear on what your responsibility actually is and what it expressly is not, especially in your own mind. For instance, consider the following:

It is not your job to "make" anyone happy other than yourself. Each person is responsible for cultivating his or her own happiness. Relying on others to provide to that to you assures failure.

It is not your job to cater to anyone's whims except your own.

It's not your job to be hit.

It's not your job to be demeaned.

It's not your job to work longer than reasonable hours in a day.

It's not your job to worry, but it is your job to problem-solve and those are two very different strategies.

It's not your job to taxi people to objectively unnecessary locations just because they do not themselves have the means to get there and you do.

It's not your job to agree to everything you are expected to or asked to do. You can say "no" and the world will keep spinning (really).

It's not your job to get involved with every drama display that finds its way to you.

It's not your job to be anyone's doormat, so do not allow others to wipe their shoes on you.

It's not your job to solve the problems of others.

It's not your job to heal the world.

It's not your job to make everything comfortable or OK for everyone else at your own ongoing expense. Sometimes, people need to wallow in inconvenience in order to learn to problem-solve for themselves. Keeping others from learning this for themselves is NOT helpful to them.

Similarly, it's not your job to shield others from the consequences of their actions.

It's not your job to "fix" other people unless you gave birth to them, in which case, fix away, sistah. Just remember that many people in prison had great parents. It's not always your fault. Adults make their own choices and this includes your children.

It's not your job to do even one favor for someone that you do not want to do.

On the other hand...

It's your job to make sure your kid gets their homework done. It's not your job to do it for them so they do not learn.

It's your job to know when to say 'no' and mean it. As they say, "No" is a complete sentence and does not require additional information or justification. Just say it with a smile and move on. They will recover.

It's your job to take care of your own health and wellness. It is not someone else's job to tell you when to sleep, eat right, exercise, meditate, and hydrate.

It's your job to own and care for your own sexuality. You say when, who, how, and why. No matter what, if you're not feeling it, it doesn't happen.

It's your job to recognize and apologize when you are in the wrong and make amends if needed.

It's your job to nurture your mind, body, and spirit in healthy ways.

It's your job to protect your mind, body, and spirit at all times without building walls that separate you from social and interpersonal experiences. Boundaries and walls are very different structures.

It's your job to acknowledge and honor your own feelings and emotions, but also to objectify them. Use them as a tool and do not let them turn *you* into a tool.

It's your job to make certain your inner intent matches up to your outer expression.

It's your job to define, identify, and protect your own boundaries. No one else should have to do it for you and they aren't likely to anyway.

It's your job to love fully with an open heart, but empower others to take care of themselves.

CHAPTER 7 – STEP 5: ACCESSORIZE, ACCESSORIZE, ACCESSORIZE

What are appropriate royal accessories, you might ask? Absolutely everything and anything that makes you feel Queenly. I have seen it all. Here is just a small sampling of what we have used to convey our royal presence:

Tiaras (I used to deliver the town mail in mine – true story)
The aforementioned faux baby seal stoles
Battery operated light up necklaces
Big bug movie star sunglasses
Opera gloves
Scepters
Fancy earrings
Fake tattoos
Real tattoos
Body glitter
Scads of different kinds of makeup
Capes

All manner of lacy things

Bump-its and Aquanet (remember, higher the hair, closer to Jesus!)

Wigs and hair extensions.

Feathers

Belly dance jingle-butt scarves

Bracelets (ankle and wrist)

Barefoot sandals

Sequin clothes

Prom dresses

Push up bras because the girls have glory

Fishnet and seamed stockings

Boas...

...and the list just goes on and on and on. YOU have to find what works for YOU and that will usually change from event to event. Troll all through the thrift stores, eBay, garage sales, gift stores, and just about anywhere that you can find items that wake up the Queenly spirit in you. Find your essential Queenly accessories and work'em girl. Your accessories are your tools and are there to accentuate your inherent spirit of fun, regal, and foxy.

Always remember, however, that you do not convey your Queenliness with the outside paraphernalia. That is there for YOU and no one else. If it makes YOU feel fun, beautiful, vibrant, and glowing, then it has done its job. Now, my Queenly finery mostly consists of great jewelry, nice make up, and flowing dresses or other clothing that I feel is flattering.

The radiance of the Queen comes from within. It is in her walk, her smile, in the twinkle of her eyes, and in the power that radiates from her. What is the sexiest thing a woman can ever wear into the room? It does not matter what her size might be, her age, her social status, her marital status, her education level, her height, or her job description. The sexiest thing a woman can wear into the room *is her self-confidence*. FIND YOURS AND FLAUNT IT!

CHAPTER 8 – STEP 6: TREAT YOUR LOYAL SUBJECTS WELL – THE *LOYAL* ONES

The controversial minister, Joel Osteen, put forth the following premise that really shook the foundation of how I distribute my energy to others. He said something to the extent of the following (paraphrasing like mad):

Of all of the people you meet, a good 25% simply are not going to like you no matter what you do. You can't make them like you by being a better person or lavishing attention onto them. You cannot love them enough or pamper them enough for them to care about you.

Another 25% are not going to like you at all, but can be convinced to like you with tremendous effort. You can work and work and over time, they will come around to thinking you are an okay person. They can, however, be easily swayed into not liking you again given the appropriate encouragement. It will be easier to convince them not to like you than it is to convince them to like you, but it can be done.

Another 25% are going to like you just fine from the beginning, but are at risk for not liking you as soon as things fail to go their way in the dynamic. When others speak poorly of you or you do something they do not appreciate, they can change their minds, but for the most part, they think you are a good sort.

The final 25% will love you no matter what and are loyal to a fault. They will be your tried and true boon companions and will defend you and love you at all costs.

Now I am not going to validate Reverend Osteen's statistics there and I would even go so far to say he may have pulled them right out of his butt to make a point rather than basing any of them on studies conducted under true scientific method. OK, he *probably* pulled them out of his butt, but you know, I have to say that my own personal experience has shown me nothing at all to doubt what he says.

He went on to point out that so often in life, we spend a huge majority of our time chasing after that 50% of people who really do not give a crap about us. Half of those people we can never convince to like us and the other half, we have to work hard to get them to like us, and then it is fragile and fickle at best.

Yet that is where our energy goes...to convince the people who do not like us that we are worthwhile.

We take advantage of the other 50%; those people who like and love us easily. We trust that they will wait around while we greedily pursue that other 50% and convince them that we are worthy of their attention.

What we should do instead is turn our backs on those who do not like us and give that attention fully to those who do. It is not a failing of the other 50%. It's not anyone's fault if the chemistry is not there for a solid and healthy connection. It just *is*. It does not necessarily make them bad people. It just *is*.

Regardless, we must turn our attention to those who love us and withdraw our energy from those who do not, for whatever reason. We must find our peace without receiving love from a full 100% of the population and instead plug in fully to our wonderful 50% who support us and love us no matter what. All of our attention, love, affection, and nurturing should go into them.

Make NO mistake: when the Queen begins to show through in you and you really are walking the talk, *people are going to notice.* No, they are not going to make fun of you and it is exactly that kind of negative thinking that break your queen persona. Well, some of them might make fun of you, but who the hell cares? Go back up and re-read, "Step 2 – Don't You Even Believe Them" if you still feel twingy about someone taking you to task over being a Queen, then say out loud to yourself, "Meh. Screw'em." Then put on your very best Cruella DeVille smile and walk that puppy coat out onto the street and show'em how we do it downtown.

You will have a certain glow to you that radiates confidence and draws people into your bubble. You can see it clearly on Queen Kathy in the photo at the beginning of this chapter. The allure is undeniable. This happens no matter what shape or size you come in because it's all about feeling good in your own skin. Expect to get many hugs, many people talking to you out of the blue, and lots of attention in general. You will draw people to you like flies to honey.

Treat those people who are drawn to you with grace and love. When people want to do things for you, compliment you, or give you gifts (yes, they will give you gifts – seriously), *smile and say thank you*. When you catch yourself saying non-Queenly tthings like, "Oh you shouldn't have…" or "I couldn't accept…" or "Truly, I can do this myself…" stop in your tracks, smile your brightest, prettiest smile, and say, "Why thank you so much!" People LOVE to do good things for Queens and will often clamor to do so. Remember those men chasing our parade float? Be ready!

Gently ease away from the people who do not contribute positively to your life. It doesn't mean you can't like or even love them, but draw back in the attention and energy you give to them. Re-establish the dancing distance between you. It does not have to be a big production. You can do it without saying a word. Pull back your energy and just don't make yourself as available as you usually are to them. Imagine that they are a nursing toddler who needs to wean. You're out of milk and then need to move on to solid food and *that's not you*. Send those little weasels off to find their own food. They can handle it. When they find the milk has dried up, they will usually move along on their own quietly, leaving you free to dote on your adoring minions.

Oh and don't worry. Even with all of lavished attention from those who love you, you can still have quiet time if you need it. Make time to give your adoring subjects their due, but then dismiss them so that you can have your alone, reflective time as well.

One of the comments I hear most about our beautiful Queens is, *"There is just something about you!"* Queens draw people to them with their radiant beauty and confident demeanor; even those who ordinarily would not be considered classic beauties. Men and women alike want to be close to them and to have the honor of doing things for them to make them smile.

The moment you question your worthiness of this attention, you've blinked. You have to keep the Queen persona fed in order for it to stay alive. To be Queen, you must truly feel your Queenliness way down to your bones and the primary component of that feeling is the knowledge that you are someone who everyone else wishes they could be.

Queens always look at though they have a secret that is so delicious, everyone else would do anything to find out what it is. A Queen always smiles broadly and walks in the conviction that she is the most beautiful creature ever to touch feet to the earth. Her eyes twinkle. Her heart soars. Her laugh is contagious. It does not matter one iota how much she weighs, how much money she has, or how much power she swings in the world. It's all in the walk, the smile and the attitude. That takes practice.

Expect to receive attention from men and honestly, sometimes, they will not know why they are attracted to you; only that they are. Your confidence and the joy you emanate will draw them in without you even trying. It takes time to get the full confidence going, but put on your Queenly airs and walk that talk *long* before you have it down pat. The more you do it, the easier it will become. Say your affirmations and remind yourself and the world that you are a Queen and *you do not take shit*. Tell yourself that you welcome the joy, happiness, and respect that you so richly deserve. Stand up taller and smile bigger, letting it travel all the way up to your eyes. Even if you feel the quivers of doubt inside, *never let'em see you sweat*. Wear your Queenly pride in every step, in every move of your hips, and in every wave of your hand. Make it so and it will be so. Create the life you want and create the confidence you want. It does not come from the outside. It starts within and then the energy moves out into the world and takes form. Your confidence and your acceptance of blessings in your life are the seeds that will grow a beautiful garden that manifests in your outside world and in your own heart.

Oh and for the record, the three handsome gentlemen in the photos used in this chapter are in no way related to Queen Kathy and had never met her before that night. She was a face in the crowd and they were drawn to her because of the power and the pleasure she radiates. Now, I promise you, they will never forget her.

CHAPTER 9 – STEP 7: LOSE THE IDEA THAT THIS IS A COMPETITION

Being a Queen is not a contest and it's not like *Highlander* where there can only be one. There is room for everyone woman to be Queen of SOMETHING and even room for many Queens to be Queen of the same thing. The fact is that if you are confident enough, other Queens will not be a threat to you at all and in fact, you will enjoy their company and they yours.

Because Queens are not threatened or insecure, the usual baseline cat fighting that occurs amongst the lesser evolved women in society simply does not happen. Everyone is secure and comfortable and this allows Queens to relax and laugh and have fun, knowing that everyone there is honoring one another as the royalty they are. This is why we can so enthusiastically go out into the world and make all the willing women we meet into Queens without it compromising our own Queenliness. It makes us all better people and takes away the nasty edge that contaminates so many female relationships. When we feel good about ourselves, other women who also feel confident are a *treat,* not a *threat.* Time to lose the "h."

Anyone who has spent time being a woman, know that women often behave abysmally to one another. In the past, before I was a Queen and met other Queens, I would actually say that I did not enjoy the company of women for just that very reason. The worst treatment I have ever endured has been at the vicious hands of other women.

All that being said, however, it is wrong to malign the entirety of any one group based on the bad behavior of a few or even many of its members. Those who say, "Men are dogs!" have simply not met the right men and likely are in a cycle dynamic that causes them to attract the same type of man over and over. The same is true for the female friends we attract. Just because a few women are bitches in no way means that they are all bitches. It just means that YOU are hanging out with bitches. There are some amazing, delicious, delightful men out there and *I completely guarantee it!* There are some loving, committed, fiery, Amazonian, warrior woman friends out there too and *I completely guarantee that as well.* It's all about the energy we put out into the world with our thoughts, words, and deeds. When we begin truly to act like Queens, those lovely women who deserve our company begin to appear in our lives like beautiful stars on the horizon.

We have no need to hurt one another, insult one another, gossip about one another, out-class, out-talk, out-rank, out-flirt, or out-smart one another. *It's not a contest.* What we do need to do is to love, support, uplift, inspire, and defend one another with our dying breaths. As Queens, we are sovereign sisters. You screw with one of us and you screw with all of us.

If there are women in your life to whom you cannot give honor and loyalty, then they need to go. The truest measure of where a person is in your life is how you feel when you are walking away from them. Do you feel somewhat dirty after you have been with them? Do you feel drained? Do you feel used? Do you feel manipulated? Do you feel shamed? Do you feel unworthy? Do you feel loved? Do you feel radiant? Do you feel invigorated? Do you feel excited? Do you feel supported? Do you feel empowered?

Take note of the feelings you experience when you interact with the other females in your world. What alliances feel healthy and supportive? What alliances feel toxic and destructive? Do what you need to do.

Remember the lesson from Chapter 7. Distancing does not have to be a huge dramatic production. You can choose to let phone calls go to voice mail from time to time. You can discover that you are busy when they call for your attention or your company. You can limit your contact to times when you know you can shield yourself from the draining impact.

That frees up time and energy for you to focus on those people in your life who *are* supportive, empowering, and worthy of your attention. Immersing yourself in the company of people who are stimulating and uplifting is the true hallmark of living a Queenly life.

CHAPTER 10 – STEP 8: PUT THE OXYGEN MASK ON YOURSELF FIRST

For this chapter, I chose to use a photo of myself from back when I was first embracing my Queenliness. I was not yet there, but I was working hard at the process. This has been one of the hardest lessons for me to learn personally and so I felt I should clean up my side of the street by making myself the poster child for not allowing oneself to deplete to the point of resentment. I can be quite the martyr, unfortunately.

How do we avoid that trap? By standing our ground. I am easily shifted into negotiation and my kids all use that against me if I am not vigilant. I admit that I am still not a master of keeping my boundaries stable without occasional compromise, but in that regard, the person I am now and the person I was when this photo was take are leagues apart. I have made remarkable progress.

The bottom line is, *They Can Handle It.* The truest heart of the issue, however, is, *can we?* Many of us wrap up a tremendous amount of our ego and our self-worth in being indispensible to other people and knowing how to solve any problem that arises. We put ourselves "on call" 24/7 and dedicate our lives to being of service to others. Letting go of that and forcing ourselves to invest in our own worth aside from what we can do for people can be challenging and terrifying. Our value does not begin and end with what we can produce and what services we can perform. We are worthwhile people inside as well and it is essential that we learn to embrace that value in ourselves. If we do not, others never will.

We do not have to try so hard all the time to be what others want us to be. We can be who we are and reclaim our time and energy to serve ourselves as well as others. We do not have to give everything within and without of us away. Sometimes, we even mortgage the incoming energy away as well. We not only can, *but must* keep some for ourselves. We can do things for ourselves. We must stand in that entitlement even when others want to take it from us because it is not convenient to them.

So how do we say no? Easy. We just say, "No." As mentioned before in this book, it is a complete sentence and needs no explanation. You can also say, "I'm not in a position to do that right now" and then lovingly disengage from the conversation if coercion ensues (and often, it will). Be wary of using phrases that invite negotiation such as, "That is not a good time for me," ("Oh, then how about later in the afternoon? Tomorrow?) or "I don't feel good about doing that" ("Then what can I do to make you feel good about it?").

Oprah Winfrey has a particular diversionary tactic she uses when she does not want to do something for someone. She says, "I need to pray about this and I will give you an answer later." She then comes back later and regretfully says, "Jesus said no."

I am more direct than that and do not get Jesus to do my dirty work. I take ownership for my own wants and needs and just say 'no.'

The biggest fear I hear is, "If I say 'no' to people, they will not like me anymore." This means that you do not trust yourself to be valuable enough to another person for who you are. You are rated and measured by what you can do for them. This is not a healthy dynamic in a relationship. If they stop liking you because you cannot cater to their whims, it was not a healthy friendship to begin with and letting them go frees up space for both of you to allow better friendships to form with others.

Saying 'no' is tough, especially if you always say 'yes.' It is a strange shift for everyone concerned and do not be surprised if you get some stunned looks in response to your rejection. Even if you say 'no' with love, there may still be some uncomfortable moments while the other person adjusts to your rejection and even more so when they realize you are not going to change your mind.

Again, do not negotiate unless you have your own terms to offer such as, "I am not going to take you to the mall today, but I can when I am already in town next Tuesday. That is what I have to offer."

A side note regarding the greatest offenders in this game: children. Our kids, of course, are usually completely dependent on us to get *anywhere* and so often, we fall into the habit of driving them wherever they wish to go simply because they have no other option. The other option is that they do not get to go and instead, stay *in our house with us* making us miserable with pouting. Stay strong. It is true that you may have to go through some of those times in order to get the *very, very vital* message to your kids that,

"Hey, my time and my wants are important too!" Releasing humans out into the world who believe that everyone will drop what they are doing to accommodate their wishes is quite a dangerous path to follow.

Just say 'no' with love and stick to it. Ignore the pangs of guilt you feel and press forward, confident that you have defended your boundaries and honored yourself as you should.

Queens have a "talk to the hand" setting that activates when they have made their point. Learn what it feels like when you have given your answer and you are finished talking about it. "I've said my piece and counted to three" is another great way of saying, "This conversation is over and there is no negotiation." Never be afraid to stand your ground and defend your boundaries. You would be surprised how well children and even spouses can take 'no' as an answer and emerge from the experience basically unscathed. When they are not used to hearing it, they may balk at first, but just watch their little faces as you remain firm with your answer and simultaneously bathe them with love and acceptance. Even if they do throw a fit, remember that fits don't kill people. Just let them know that you will be available for their apology when they are finished. This techniques works on both adults and children *just fine*.

The real trick is to refrain completely from further conversation, negotiation, deliberation, compromise, discussion, argument, defense, or explanation. Give your answer and leave it at that. Be loving, but firm. Do not negotiate with terrorists, at least not at first. As you find your feet in Queenliness, it will be easier to compromise without releasing your personal power. When you are just starting out, let it be okay to stay firm on your decision and not give an inch. You have that right and you are not, *not,* a bad person for sticking to your guns. When you have worn your crown for a while and gotten the feel of the process, then you can tackle the intricate nature of compromise.

What we are doing when we embrace our Queenliness is actually changing relationship dynamics, both with others and with ourselves. We establish patterns and power distribution patterns with every relationship in our lives. When we shift that dynamic without the other person's consent, they often feel out of balance and sometimes even victimized. Don't worry. They will regain their footing again and get used to the new energy. It will take a little time, but as long as you integrate your life changes with love and consistency, the new "normal" will take over and you will find that the overall response is likely favorable once the adjustment period completes.

As you begin to implement your new Queenly life, you will naturally find that some relationships are unable to survive the transition. I guarantee you that the changes you see occur are in everyone's best interest. Those around you who thrive on drama, gossip, malicious behavior, passive-aggressive bullshit, manipulation, emotional usury and blackmail, back-stabbing, and humiliation will slip away as they see those practices no longer yield them the desired results with you. This will make your life cleaner and more enjoyable.

If no one else has ever told you, I am going to tell you right now: *You have the right to be happy. You have the right to experience joy, fulfillment, and satisfaction in your life.* You do not have to sacrifice those rights just so you can be at the disposal of others. This theme repeats throughout this book simply because some people do not hear it enough.

If you have been a person who historically gives over your will to others and sacrifices your own desires for the wants of others *every time*, then now is the time for you to step out of that martyrdom cave and into the sunlight. YOU are just as important as anyone else is and stepping forward to claim your own joy is your *birthright*. You are NOT inflicting an unjustified raid or attack on others. You are reclaiming something precious that by rights belongs to you. Sure, maybe you gave it away in an effort to please, in an attempt to be important. We do this because we do not trust who we are to be *enough*. Unfortunately, when we continually over-give and over-extend, we end up on empty. It takes time, true enough, but eventually, we all end up there: dried up, empty, resentful, and with nothing left to give anyone, least of all ourselves.

This happens because we gave away something we desperately needed to keep. We begin to feel bereft in our spirit knowing that something essential is lacking. We start to feel resentful that others are not doing for us on the level that we do for them. We begin to keep score and become frustrated that we do so much for others and receive so little in return.

The only way to correct the situation is to take back what we gave away. That is not to say we should never do anything for anyone. Far from it. Some of our greatest joys derive from giving to others and showing them we care how they feel and what they need. It is essential, however, that we keep some of our energy and essence in reserve rather than giving until we are empty and spent. We must create a life we love and that feeds *us* as well rather than working constantly on output. Even flight instructions on an airplane are clear that in case of an emergency, *put the oxygen mask on yourself first,* then help those who are unable to help themselves.

The happier we are, the more we have in our cup to give to others. Interestingly, if we keep it all for ourselves, the fluid in the cup will become stagnant and gross. The only way to maintain fresh, vibrant energy is to have an ongoing flow both in and out that is balanced. Too many of us are so out of balance that we are on the verge of or in the process of a mental and spiritual breakdown. Often, that extends to a physical breakdown as well. Our spirits, our minds, and our bodies are not intended to function in an all take or all give dynamic. It is up to us, not anyone else in the whole world, to establish and protect that flow in good balance.

Being a Queen is about creating the perfect exchange of energy in and energy out and honoring it at all times. It is about giving to others with grace and dignity while taking our own pleasures as well. It is about knowing well our limits and remaining mindful of how our energy outflow relates to our energy reserves.

All of these are important practices that will keep you grounded, centered, and stable as a Queen. Even though you are working from a humanitarian perspective of keeping yourself nurtured so that you are better able to give to others, you may have someone, or several someones, bitching about how you just are not as "nice" as you used to be. How something about you has shifted and doesn't feel right.

Those who love you, want to see you succeed, and want to see you empowered, healthy, and happy, will embrace this new you like a duck to water. They may not *trust* it at first until you demonstrate without fail that it is going to stick, but they will support it and that is what is most important.

CHAPTER 11 – STEP 9: DO WHAT YOU LOVE AND LOVE WHAT YOU DO

As you can see from Queen Lindze's glowing smile above, sometimes, you can wear the tiara on the inside and still radiate the royal vibe. That's because it comes from living the life you truly want to live and finding passion in the things you do in your life. Begin to eliminate everything from your life that you do not love to do. Most adults responded to this idea with a huffy, "Oh it's just NOT that easy! I couldn't just *not do* blah blah blah." Yes. You. CAN. It's CHOICES! You would be surprised how many things you hate doing that you can just stop doing. Fill those spaces with the things you love to do instead. It's really that easy. Eat only the foods you love. Participate in activities that feed your spirit. Be with the people you love being around. Distance yourself from those who leave you feeling drained and sad. It really is just that easy. Everyone has reasons for why they can't make those changes. "Reasons" are often nothing more than "excuses" when examined closely. Lose the excuses and just do it. It's amazing how many times we do things we hate doing just because someone else told us we had to.

Sure, we have to clean our toilet, do our laundry, and sweep our floors unless we hire someone to do it through barter or payment. I have actually bartered with people to clean my house by offering them something I love to do in return, such as a home cooked meal, a Tarot reading, flowers, a professionally designed website, or a massage. I have asked friends to come over and talk to me while I clean my house so that even though the activity I am performing is not fun, the company is. We can find ways to sweeten the tasks we don't really want to do. We can listen to music while we jog or do it with a friend. We can listen to audio books while we drive (I hate driving).

Inevitably, there will be things we have to do that we hate and cannot sweeten to the point that they are tolerable to us. In those cases, it is best to show grace and get them done as quickly and efficiently as possible so that we can move on to other more enjoyable activities. What is important to consider is that when we fill our lives with things we love to do, the times when we must endure things we do not love to do are much more palatable. When we live a life filled with things we *do not* want to do, one more can be the straw that breaks the camel's back. It's like having a bruise on your arm. A bruise hurts when someone pokes it, but the same degree of pressure on a non-bruised arm causes no pain at all.

Find your passion and explore it.

Remember what you enjoyed doing as a child. Remember what you wanted to be when you grew up. Go back and re-collect the plans you made for yourself before life got in the way. Think about the times in your life when you have been genuinely, organically happy and note what you were doing and what was going on in your life to support that degree of joy.

You may have started to notice that many of the messages in these chapters are interlinked. Doing what you love to do and trimming out the things you do not love to do relate back to the ability to say 'no' when someone asks you to do something you do not wish to do. Protecting your boundaries and making room for joy in your life relate to loving yourself and claiming your Queenly birthright. The ability to do so without guilt touches on keeping your own side of the street clean so that you are "right with the Lord," so to speak. You should be able to live in your own skin and be proud of who you are in order to offer yourself this kind of love. Finding the love and respect for yourself sometimes comes from a "fake it 'til you can make it" approach.

There is a tall tale that says that someone once asked Michelangelo how he could carve something as beautiful as the statue of David from a block of marble.

"It was easy," the artist supposedly said. "All I did was chip away everything that didn't look like David."

Those are your marching orders right there.

Take time when you know you will not be interrupted. If you have no time *ever* when you will not be interrupted, you have already identified one problem you must correct. *Everyone* needs quiet, contemplative time. *Make* time when you will not be interrupted and quiet your thoughts. Get into a comfortable position and take deep, soothing breaths, deeper than your usual breathing. Let the breath move through you, nourishing you and feeding your body, mind, and spirit. Let all of the static and concern of the day stop for a little while. Find the stillness.

Within that stillness, begin to imagine your life as you would wish it to be. What would be different? Stretch your mind beyond your current circumstances and think about what you would like to do in your day-to-day life and in your overall life. What would you like to feel? Who would you like to have share your life with you? Imagine it clearly, as though it is already done. What would you do for a living? What hobbies would you explore? How would you spend your recreational time? Who would you love? What would you wear?

Once you have this clearly in your mind, write it out on paper or a computer file. Keep it for reference and edit it as needed, then begin the process of carving away everything that does not look like the life you envisioned.

Start off with small with subtle changes, but keep the bigger changes in mind and in focus. Welcome those changes into your life. Gradually, create the life you want to live so that you love what you do and do what you love.

It sounds daunting and it truly is an act of courage, but then, Queens have to be bold and brave and make life choices that support the monarchy. So should you.

CHAPTER 12 - STEP 10: ABOVE ALL, GO FOR THE FUN

Princess Diana of Wales showed the whole world (and the monarchy) that the worst thing royalty could do is to take itself too seriously. She was elegant and beautiful and the perfect princess, but she and Princess Sarah Ferguson also poked people in their butts with umbrellas. Princess Dianna was regal, fabulous, and so well loved, but she did not give a crap about the stodgy rules that others foisted upon her. She took the concept of royalty and made it her own and in doing so, created a dynasty that lives on in her sons.

How sad to live life with an agenda of filling your days with tasks you hate to perform and feelings of inadequacy about yourself. Society sets us up impossible body images and career aspirations for us to reach. Refuse that trap! You have the power to balance your life with happiness and confidence. You can create the life you want to live *right now*. Do not hold your joy hostage until you lose a certain amount of weight, get a particular job, get a specific academic grade, or find the perfect love. Your perfect love is the love you have for yourself and the greatest success you can ever know is in cherishing yourself and fully appreciating the unique and glorious individual that you are. All other successes flow from that source. Just saying positive words about yourself can start the process. "I am gorgeous just as I am." "I am a precious person." Fake it 'til you can make it. It WILL make a difference.

Love yourself above, *yes, above* all others. Love yourself and show your children how to love themselves. Teach your daughters that they are princesses and as princesses, they have responsibilities to themselves and to others. Teach your kids how to have fun and cut loose from the bonds of what society expects them to be.

Find your own fun where you can. Take your pleasure where you can. We must savor life, not just endure it. As a grown adult, you have the right and the responsibility to welcome pleasure into your life as a lifestyle. Embrace your sexuality with tremendous relish and savor who you are sexually. Delve into the spiritual practice that calls you and find spiritual ecstasy. Revel in the beauty of nature and the sweetness and nurturing deliciousness of food. Surround yourself with people who lift you up and celebrate who you are, with people who inspire you, motivate you, and accept you for who you truly are. Find the people who love you for who you are in your most authentic self; not people who love you *in spite of who you are.*

Love your body, just as it is. Think of all of the abuse it has taken through in the years you have been alive and how it is still there for you. Look into the mirror and do not stop until you see your inner beauty hiding inside there. Make a list of the qualities that make you loveable and add to it every day. Do things every day that make you smile and bring you closer to who you truly are and who you want to be some day. Advance your life on a regular basis toward your goals. Step out of your comfort zone to do things for yourself. Give yourself love and acceptance until you can draw in others who will as well. Say wonderful things about yourself every day.

Find the fun. Figure out what you love to do and then rock that shit. Immerse yourself in joyful activities and find your bliss. It's there. I promise.

Live every day in such a way that people wonder what on earth it is that gives you so much happiness. BE the Queen of your life and really, truly, *accept nothing less*. This is not something you are stealing from the world. It is something you gave away or that was taken from you that you must recover in order to live a whole and fulfilling life.

The only thing worse than living as long as you have without being a Queen...without being *The Queen*, is living one more day without being The Queen.

Now...What Does Her Majesty Desire?

ABOUT THE AUTHOR

Katrina Rasbold has provided insightful guidance to countless individuals over the past three decades through both her life path consultations and her informative classes and workshops. She has worked with teachers all over the world, including three years of training in England and two years of practice in the Marianas Islands. She is a professional life coach who holds a Ph.D in Religion. She is married and she and her husband, Eric, co-authored the Bio-Universal Energy book series.

Katrina lives in the forested Eden of the High Sierras of Northern California near Tahoe. Katrina is a hermit who lives inside her beautiful mountain home, pecking away at her computer keyboard. She frequently teaches workshops on different aspects of Bio-Universal energy usage in the El Dorado, Sacramento, and Placer counties of California. She has six children, two teens at home and four who are grown up and out there loose in the world.

OTHER BOOKS BY THE AUTHOR
(Available on Amazon.com)

Where the Daffodils Grow

The Daughters of Avalon

Rose of Avalon

The Dance Card

Energy Magic

Energy Magic Compleat

Beyond Energy Magic

CUSP

Properties of Magical Energy

Reuniting the Two Selves

Magical Ethics and Protection

The Art of Ritual Crafting

The Magic and Making of Candles and Soaps

Days and Times of Power

Crossing The Third Threshold

How to Create a Magical Working Group

An Insider's Guide to the General Hospital Fan Club Weekend

Leaving Kentucky in the Broad Daylight

The Real Magic

Get Your Book Published

Goddess in the Kitchen: The Magic and Making of Food

Spiritual Childbirth

Tarot For Real People

OTHER QUEENLY RESOURCES YOU MUST INVESTIGATE

The Sweet Potato Queens Book of Love by Jill Conner Browne

Queen of Your Own Life by Kathy Kinney and Cindy Ratzlaff

Queenisms: 100 Jolts of Inspiration by Kathy Kinney and Cindy Ratzlaff

The Sweet Potato Queens' Guide to Life by Jill Conner Browne

The Sweet Potato Queens' Field Guide to Men by Jill Conner Browne